AMAZING ABC GIRLS

I0171137

COLOR ON!

The Alliterative Athlete's Coloring Book

by
D. M. Kilian

Amazing ABC Girls Color On!
The Alliterative Athlete's Coloring Book

Coloring companion to picture book
Amazing ABC Girls Game On!

Copyright © 2017 D. M. Kilian

All rights reserved. No portion of this book may be reproduced in any form without the express written permission of the copyright holder. For permission contact:

art@kinematicpress.com
www.kinematicpress.com

First Edition

ISBN-13: 978-0-9994482-1-2
ISBN-10: 0-9994482-1-8

Kinematic Press
Redwood City, CA

This coloring book
belongs to:

_____

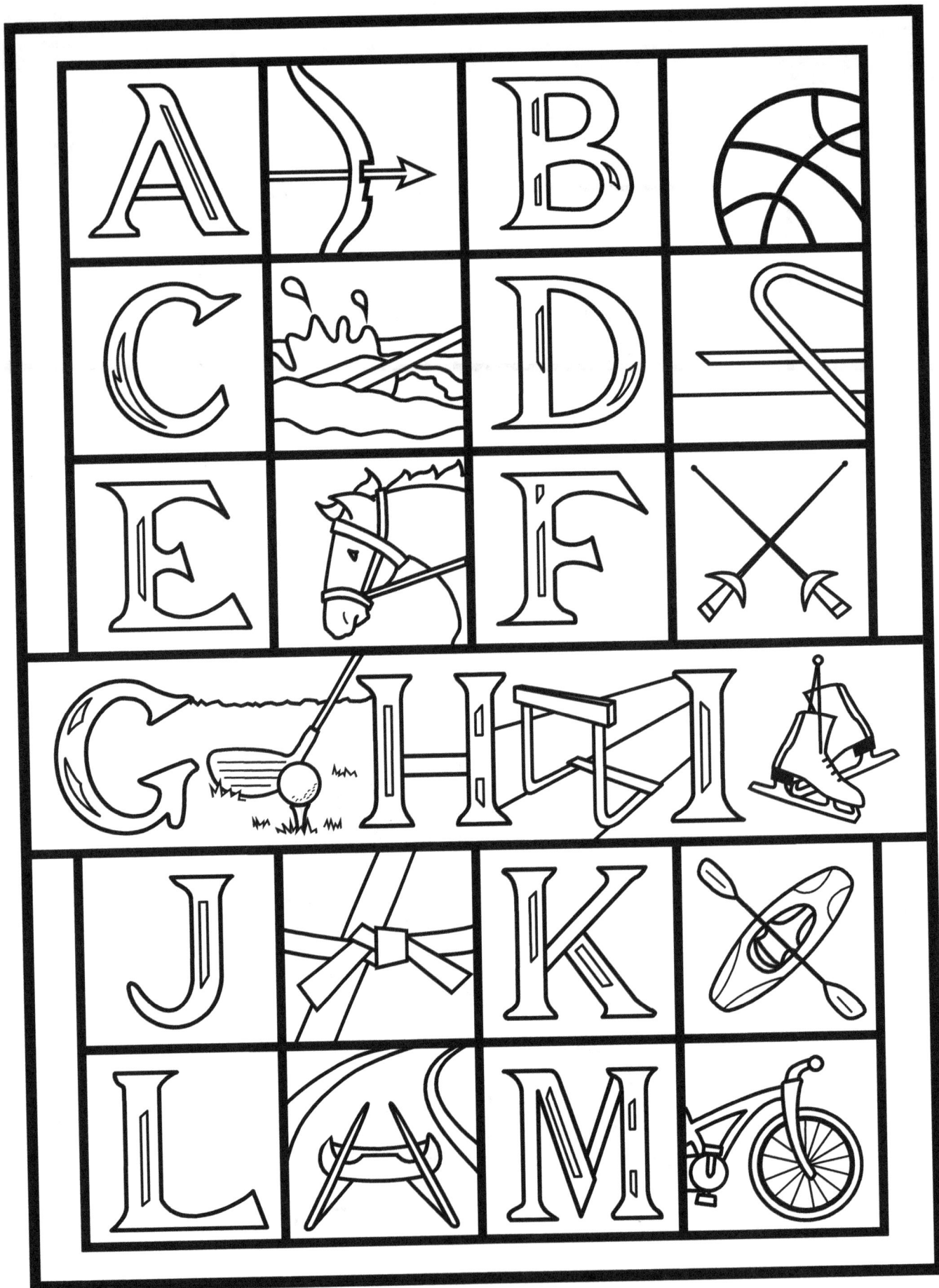

Pick a sport, grab your gear ...

...and start coloring the Amazing ABC Girls!

Amy takes aim at the archery range.

Brianna bounds up for a basket.

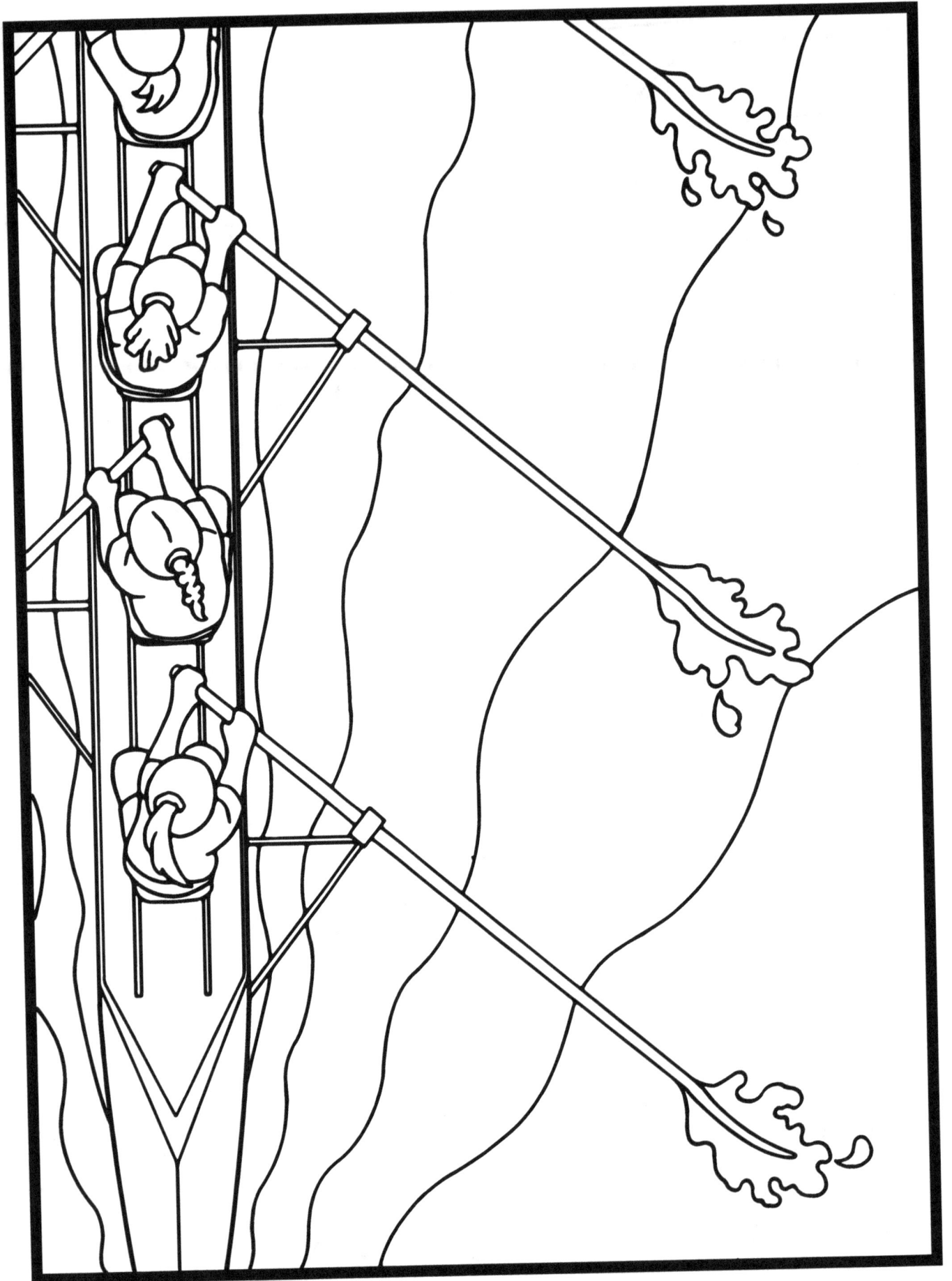

Competing crews can't catch Carmen & Co.

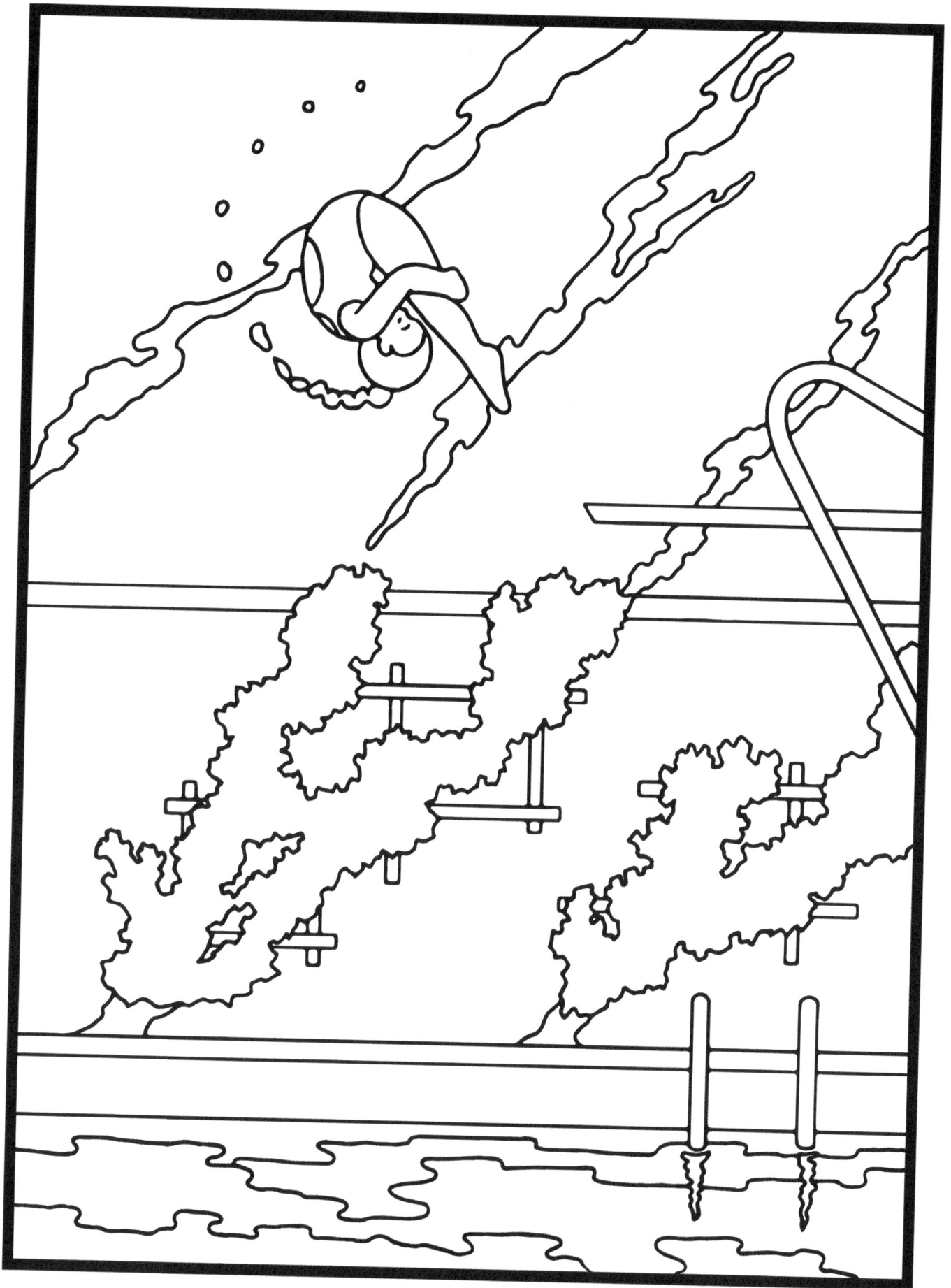

Dana dares to dive daily.

Equestrian Emma endorses horses.

Fencing is Fayza's favorite.

Gwen is game for golf.

Hey Hailey, how about hurdles?

Isabel is into ice skating.

Joy and Judy, judo jocks.

Keiko has a knack for kayaking.

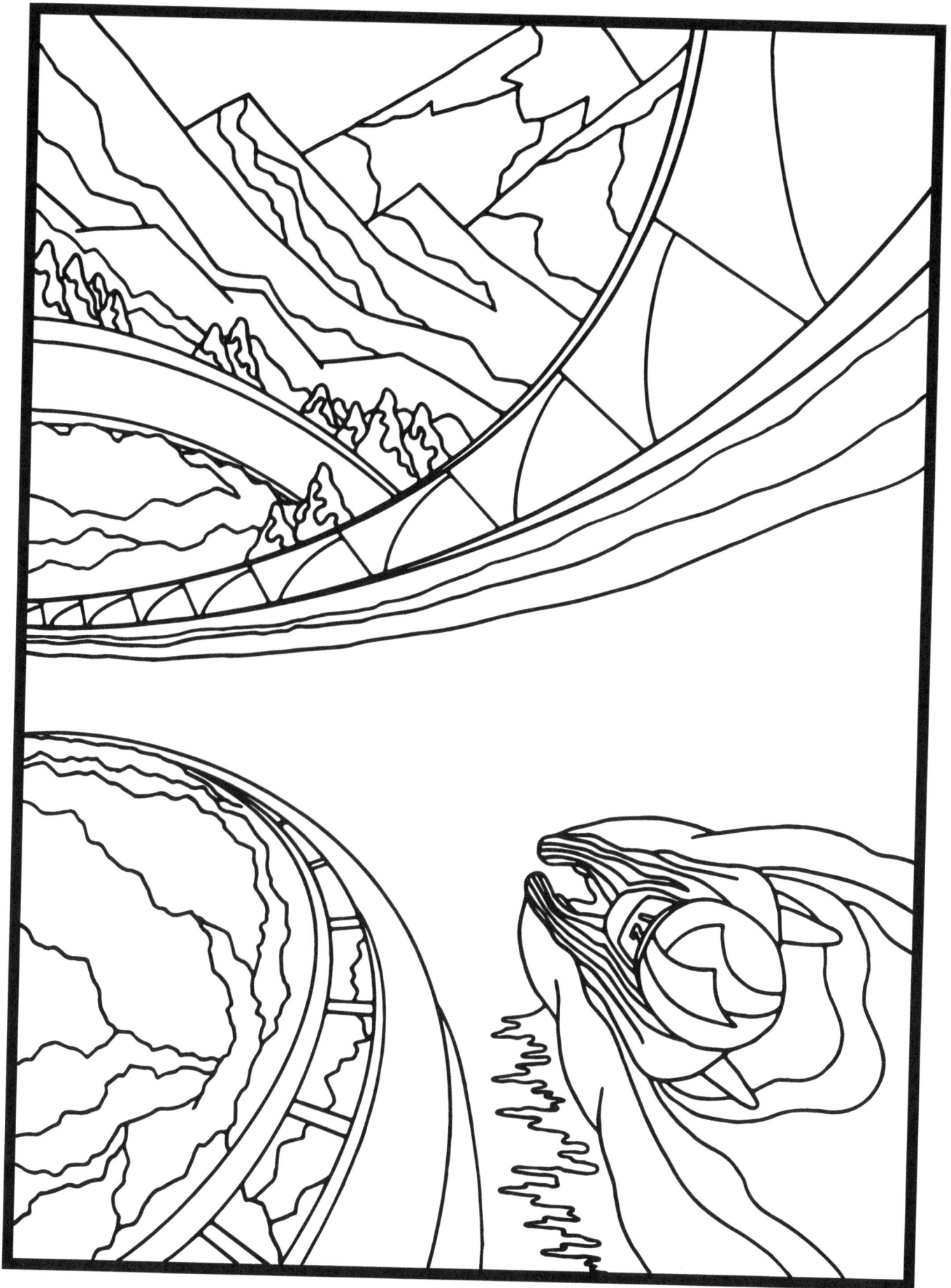

Lydia loves her luge for speed.

Ming-mei masters mountain biking.

Nancy and Nora are Nordic naturals.

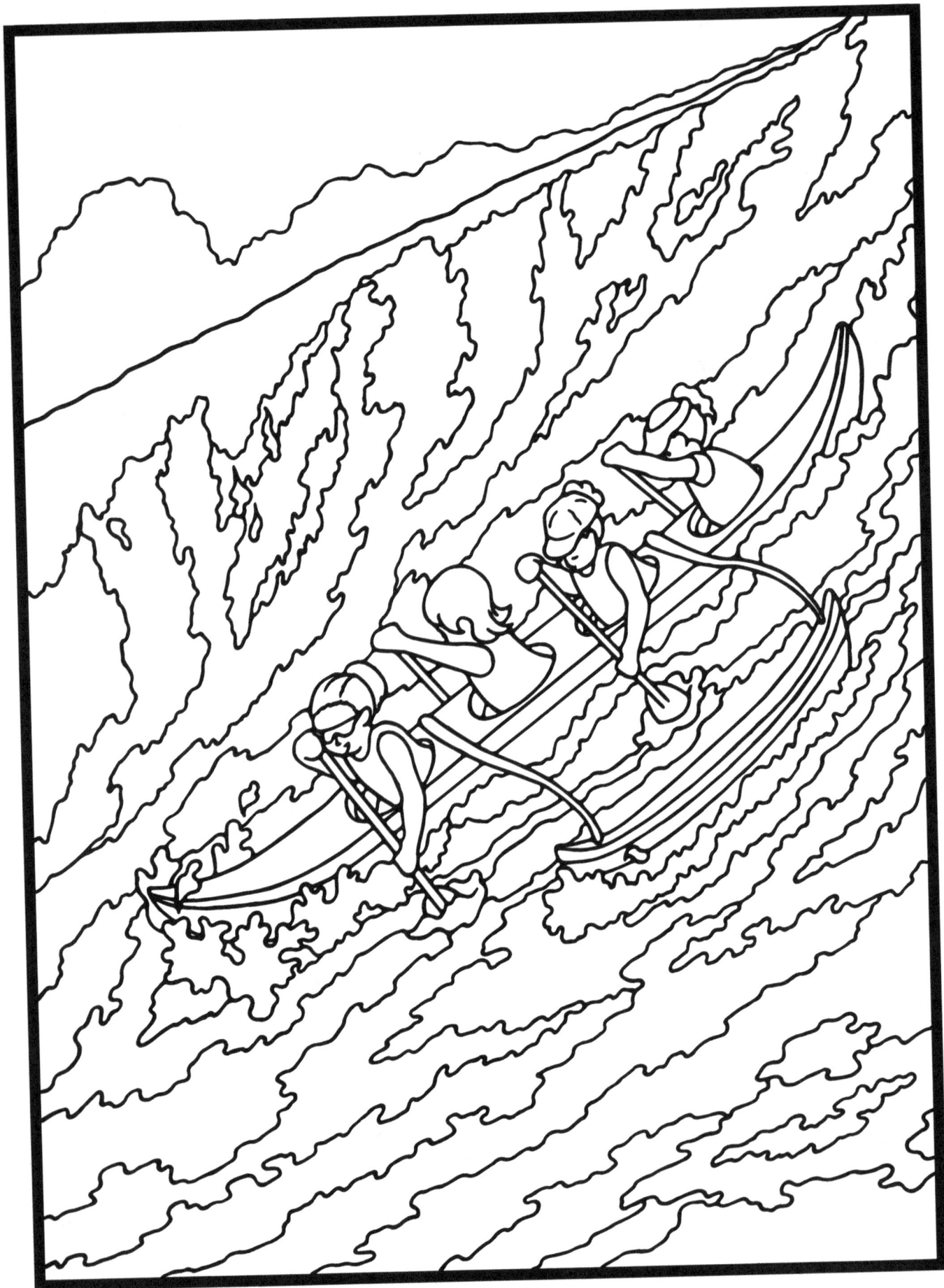

Olga opts for outrigger canoeing.

Pole vaulting is Paula's pick.

Queena acquaints herself with quoits.

Rhonda & Rikki rule the rocks.

Suvi scores with soccer.

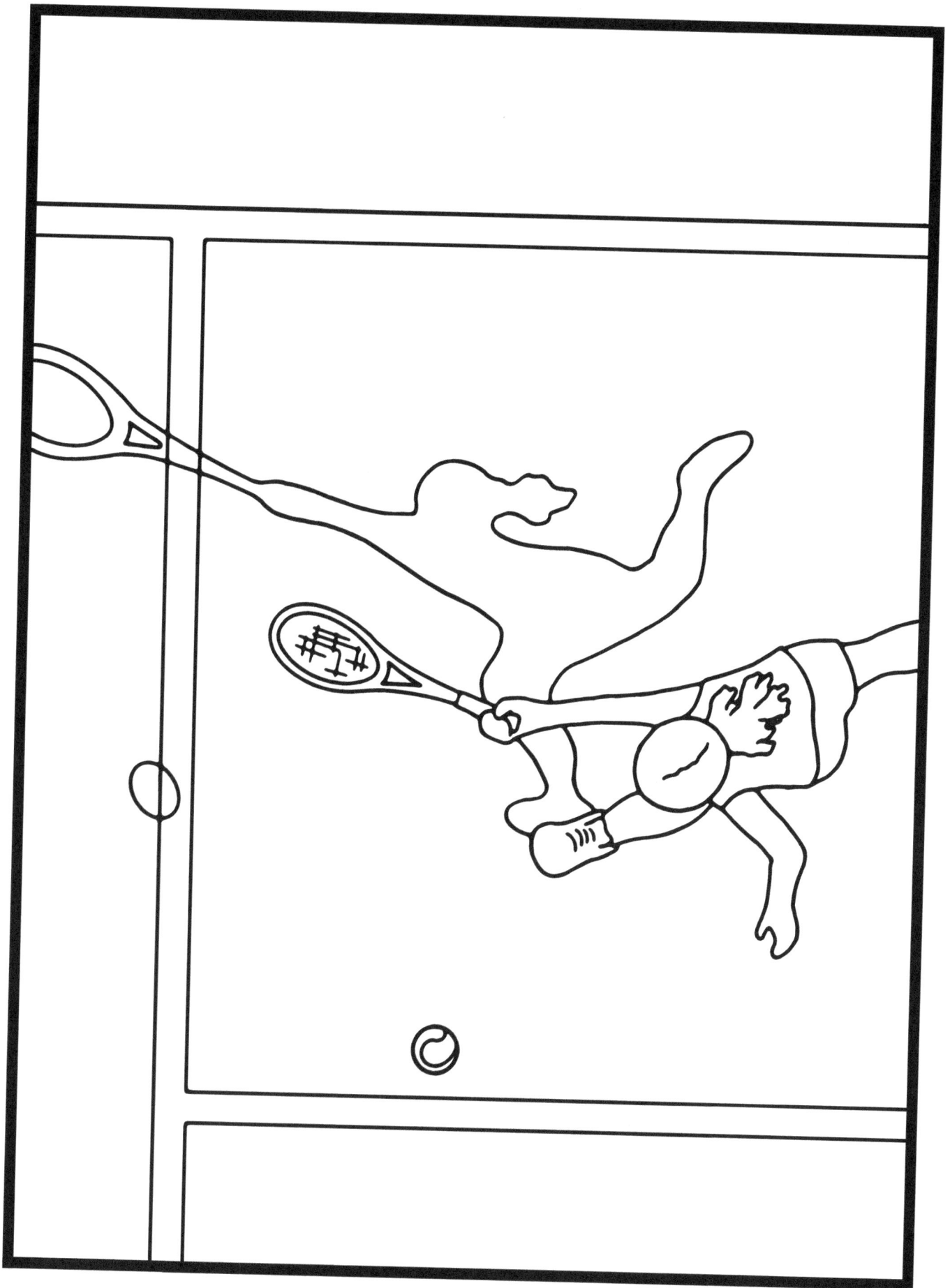

Tanisha triumphs at tennis.

Uma unearths the ultimate sport.

Volleyball is Vicky's favorite.

Wanika windsurfs the waves.

Xandra excels at everything eXtreme.

Yolanda says "yes" to yoga.

Zelda is a zipline zealot.

www.ingramcontent.com/pod-product-compliance
Lightning Source LLC
Chambersburg PA
CBHW080536030426
42337CB00023B/4762